RUNNING FROM THE

HEART

RUNNING FROM THE

HEART

JEANNIE LONG

To order additional copies of this book, contact:
Xlibris
1-888-795-4274
www.Xlibris.com
Orders@Xlibris.com
768111

Your legacy lives on!

In loving memory of our precious and beloved children:

Rebecca Long
January 22, 1982 — May 8, 2014

Alexander Derry Long (Alex)
December 13, 1987 — November 8, 2005

I imagine Rebecca might say something like, "Run the race with all your heart, it will be worth it, you cannot imagine how wonderful it is here."

Heartfelt Thanks

I give God the glory, although weary from grieving,
you helped me up to be more than I could be!

To Gerard, my husband, my best friend, you fought for me, you never let go of God or me, bringing me back from the brink by going to the throne room of grace. Thank you, with all the pieces of my broken heart, I'm better with hugs and kisses because your love really means more than my words can say. You are the love of my life and truly the greatest Dad to Rebecca, Ben and Alex.

Thank you for bringing order to Running from the Heart. We both know I could not have done this without you. As we worked together through my tears and, "I can't do this," neither of us found this healing, as some might think. Only because of you, we kept moving forward and although very slowly, you were very patient, cheering and encouraging me on. You are the best encourager I know.

To my precious son Ben, I'm so proud to be your mum, and I love you more than words can say. You have walked through so much; your strength and courage inspire me. I love your heart to want to help others, and thank you for your encouragement to finish the devotional.

To my dearest friends, I am humbled to call you my sweet sisters. My very heartfelt gratitude for sustaining me with your amazing love, prayers, support and encouragement, at just the right moment, which I can only describe as supernatural, with coffee and cookies somewhere in the mix – Jami, Jenny, Lani, Judy, Lena, Jill, Susan, Elissa, Stephanie, Tina, Page, Angelika, Kim, Gloria, Elaine, Lachele, Cathy, Lisa, Joanie, Jackie and Julie.

To our precious and God given partners in the ministry, Anand and Sheen. We deeply appreciate your friendship, diligence and skills.

To our editorial team: Anand, Sheen, Maddie, Jesse and Michele.

Special heartfelt thanks to Grandma Marion and Grandma Bridget.

Thanks to all the lovely friends who have prayed for and supported Running from the Heart.

Thank you to all Rebecca's friends who made her life so rich and full of love and laughter.

Thank you to all of Rebecca's Alpha friends, work colleagues, youth pastors and ministry leaders – she loved being co-workers for God's Kingdom with you all.

And, I know Rebecca would want us to give a shout out to her three Alpha Youth Board members – Jamie, Lani and Brock. She deeply appreciated your friendship, wisdom and prayers.

Contents

Foreword

The book you hold in your hands tells the story of a remarkable young woman, my beloved friend Rebecca Long. She was extremely gifted in all of the ways the world measures: physical beauty, intelligence, athletic ability and very kind and welcoming to everyone she encountered. Her world was drawn to her. Yet none of these gifts held Rebecca. As you will read in these pages, Rebecca's identity was rooted solely in who she was in Jesus Christ. Her passion was to boldly share his love which she did everywhere she went, and sometimes she used words.

I met Rebecca in 2002 when her lovely family moved to Rye, New York, where my family lived. At the time, Rebecca was a university student in England. When she visited her family, she often babysat my five children, leading five bicycles through the streets of Rye and playing hours of games on the front lawn, including the English game she taught them, 'Kick the Can.' The kids never minded when my husband and I left them if Rebecca was around!

Our family moved to London in 2008, and Rebecca visited us there often while traveling for her work with Alpha Youth. These visits gave us time to discuss many things. We shared our personal journeys, hearts, and prayers as well as our workout regimens and favorite running routes. (Rebecca challenged me to try her back breaking interval sprints along Hyde Park-not easily done!)

I also discovered Rebecca's favorite cereal from Marks and Spencer which is now my favorite cereal. What precious time this was.

In 2011, Rebecca asked me to join the newly formed board for Alpha Youth, USA. It was an honor and privilege to hear what the Lord was doing through Rebecca's ministry and how clearly, He was guiding her and Alpha Youth. Her example of serving others and putting their interests first became even more evident to me. Rebecca led Alpha Youth as she led her life. She was always alert, waiting for the Lord to direct her and she allowed God to speak into the silences she intentionally carved out.

A week before Rebecca went to be with the Lord, she visited San Diego where we had moved. We had an opportunity to work together on Alpha Youth plans and catch up personally as we ran the streets and beach near our home. Rebecca shared with me about her family members and her many friends across the globe whom she loved and adored and her professional and personal goals. She was trusting the Lord for what was ahead. One week later, the day of Rebecca's passing and the day before I learned of it, I found an unusual clam shell glistening at the water's edge on the beach near where we had run together. It was pink on one side and white on the other and on the pink side had ridges running down its surface. There was the profile of a small face on its upper edge, and it appeared as a ballerina with her skirt flowing. It was stunning.

I had never seen a shell like this. After hearing about Rebecca's passing, I sensed the shell was a gift from the

Lord for Jeannie. A few days later my feelings seemed confirmed when my friend Lani, who also serves on the board for Alpha Youth, called me to ask if Rebecca had been a ballerina. Lani had dreamed of Rebecca dancing as a ballerina at her wedding with the Lord. (Jeannie, Rebecca's mother, was a professional ballerina.)

One more thing about the shell. There was a smaller shell embedded into both sides of the clam, the pink and the white side, at the top where the two sides were joined. A shell on a shell. Similarly, Rebecca's life was embedded in so many others' lives, including mine.

Christmas 2010, Rebecca gave me an Oswald Chambers daily calendar devotional. One of Oswald's phrases has come to my mind over and again since Rebecca's passing. It refers to the life of service God intends for his followers: to be "broken bread and poured-out wine." Rebecca's life was exactly that. She gave her all every day for His glory. I am a blessed and grateful recipient of her grace and love and a witness to her example of what a life devoted to God looks like. Her example lives on inspiring me and everyone who had the gift of knowing her to 'run with perseverance the race marked out for us, fixing our eyes on Jesus, the pioneer, and perfecter of faith'.

I am thankful for the gift of Rebecca's friendship and trust that the words of this devotional will encourage and inspire its readers to want to know and follow the Jesus Rebecca followed and to want to share this book with family and friends.

Jami Voge

Introduction

Heart to Heart

Running from the Heart is a testimony of a life well lived. Through tragic necessity, Rebecca's life inspires new beginnings from a heart redeemed by Christ.

Rebecca may only be a name to you, but she was our precious daughter and sister to Ben and Alex. Through my broken heart, I am humbled and privileged to share her sweet love for Jesus through her journal entries.

Glimpses in Rebecca's journal speak of a young woman of faith. During the last eight years of her life, she writes tenderly of her sorrow and joy in the unexplained ways of God, when her life had been turned upside down. She kept her eyes on Jesus, no matter what. Her thoughts, running freely, focused on Him.

She was clearly refreshed in her soul by Gods word and many sweet passages are included in her journals. With a humble heart, she went from strength to strength and showed the world the loveliness of Jesus Christ. Although Rebecca's heart was very broken and she had many struggles, she triumphed in life with a sweetness and joy of the Lord. She wrote,
I choose joy.

Rebecca made the decision to give her heart to Jesus at 11 years old, for time and eternity. Her baptism was so precious to her daddy and me. Our hearts were deeply touched as we looked proudly at Rebecca with the family present and her friends, sitting in the front row.

I'll never forget, after the pastor thanked Rebecca for her testimony, she said, *"Oh no! I have more to share."* She was so full of what Jesus meant to her, she burst into the most heavenly song I have ever heard. Her soul running on the wings of forever, He had put a new song in her heart. Rebecca was the happiest girl.

In one of her last journals, she wrote,
Faith, it is rather like running in a race.

At times her race was hard. Life is hard! Yes, she stumbled but she was committed and remained loyal, persevering with the truth of her hearts conviction. She went from strength to strength, as a champion runner, a champion of the faith.

In my dream, I hear them calling her beautiful name, "Rebecca! Rebecca! Come on Rebecca!"

The crowd, cheering her on, set the stadium on fire, baton in hand she ran her race to victory.

Our darling Rebecca, running with all her heart!

Her dad, Gerard, and brothers, Ben and Alex, always louder than most, made me smile as I looked on with pride, but always moved to tears. Not simply for her running, but the reason for running.

In her heart, Rebecca witnessed to her faith in Christ through her running. God had made her fast and when she ran, she felt His pleasure. Ever since she had seen Chariots of Fire (one of her favorite films), she made the quote her own, "when I run, I feel His pleasure."

She had a big dream of running in the Olympics, to give God the Glory. With hard work and perseverance, she achieved a personal best time of 2:10 for the 800 meters (running very fast twice round the track). It was her favorite event and her dad's and Alex's too. She was on her way! Rebecca ran with all her heart, the race marked out for her.

God was strengthening and shaping Rebecca's heart through her running; the self-discipline she learned helped for what was to come. I watched God raise up a champion warrior of the faith. Rebecca wrote,

What I learned as an athlete, prepared me for such a time as this.

Out of the past and into the future, Rebecca is now in Heaven, her true home and with Alex, her beloved brother. They are cheering us on with the great crowd of witnesses.

Left amongst her things, I found her journals. I held them to my heart and, through the tears, I remembered our last hug. Suddenly, a piece of paper fell to the floor. It was the speech she had given at her 21st Birthday. Humbly, in front of her friends, she expressed her sweet love and gratitude to the God of all grace, and the love she felt for her family and friends – what a precious night!

After that I could not bring myself to read Rebecca's journals for a very long time but, when I did, they felt so sacred. I sensed God's presence and I have to believe I found them as part of her legacy.

Sweet Memories

These very kind words[1] reflect that Rebecca's sweet walk with Jesus had a unique and profound touch on the people who met her.

"I thought of Rebecca's work in the US and all around the world and how so many lives were and will continue to be impacted because of her faithfulness to serve Christ and others. I thought of all the seeds she had planted and how our tears in the grief of her loss will water those seeds and great fruit will arise because of her legacy."

"Rebecca had a lasting impact on my life. Never before had I met such a beautiful young lady who was also sold out for God. Her faith, kindness and strength in the midst of her own grief so impressed me that I renewed my faith and started teaching Sunday school in my local church."

"Rebecca is a role model of the type of woman I want to be. I became more inspired by her as I witnessed her unmatched faith. She helped me see what a young

---

[1]   A selection, taken from hundreds of sweet messages.

woman living for the Lord looks like and made me want to be like her."

A man once expressed to us, *"Rebecca was one of the two most holy women I had ever met!"* Because of that single encounter, he said, *"When I heard the news of her being called home, in some ways, I wasn't surprised!"* All I could think was I just want my girl back, but with his words came the thought, "for whom the world was not worthy!"

Our prayer is that Rebecca's relationship with God will inspire and encourage you to live a surrendered and abundant life for Jesus Christ. In one of her journal entries, she wrote,
Live life to the full for Jesus!

Rebecca has finished her race, passing on the baton of truth to you and may the beauty and grace of Jesus Christ reflect in your life as you run the race God has given to you.

About Rebecca

Rebecca was born on January 22nd 1982, in Hampstead, London, England. The firstborn daughter to Gerard and Jeannie Long, her very proud parents, and big sister to Ben, born April 19th 1984 and Alex born December 13th 1987. She was born into a family, who for generations had walked with Jesus.

Rebecca was almost born running from the moment she came into the world. She even told me, she preferred running to walking.

From the start, she was curious and eager to get on with life. It tells you something of her character that, not dissimilar to her namesake in the bible; Rebecca was never one to tarry, hardworking and clothed with strength, dignity and integrity. She was not only beautiful but had a kind, generous, thankful and humble heart. With a gentle and quiet confidence, she was the bravest girl we knew.

A very British girl she was mature beyond her years; a sweet daughter who honored her mum and dad. And, she adored her younger brothers.

Running – Rebecca was just 10 years old when she was scouted at a school sports event to become a runner. From that day, to the day she was called home, Rebecca ran.

Rebecca was a loyal team member of Highgate Harriers, her running club. An article in the newspaper claimed, "one of the driving forces behind the Highgate Harriers success comes in the shape of 18-year old Rebecca Long."

Dedicated to her training, she became London schools' 800m champion, Middlesex County/State champion, a champion at Bristol University and was offered a running scholarship to receive her MBA at Loyola University, Chicago, where, as a champion, she held the league record for 800m for several years. Training with professional coaches, Rebecca was on target to bring her times down to qualify for the trials for the London Olympics.

We miss watching her run. We miss her smile. We miss that swishy ponytail. We just miss her! I miss Alex too!

School/Work – St Michael's School, Highgate and, at eleven years old, she passed the entrance exam to Francis Holland School, Clarence Gate, London. Described as scholarly, Rebecca was a grade A student, who was encouraged to do the Oxbridge entrance exams (Oxford and Cambridge Universities). However, she changed direction and studied History at Bristol University, to dedicate more time to train with her coaches.

Rebecca completed her MBA at 25 years old and had been looking forward to entering the corporate world. However, during her MBA, her world fell apart when her little brother Alex (17) went home to Heaven. Through the many tears and prayers, sensing a call from God she relinquished all to invest her life in sharing her faith with young people. The Lord graciously opened a door, and she joined Alpha USA, becoming the National Director for Alpha Youth. Hard-working and passionate until the day God called her home.

Rebecca was a beautiful and strong woman, focused and not easily distracted. I remember she even turned down the offer to model in New York, not once but twice. She said to me she simply wasn't called to modelling.

I weep again as I read in one of her journals, underlined, _The most important thing in life is my relationship with God._

2005 – 2005 was a very very dark year! A year when the lights went out and everything changed. Rebecca was told she had Retinitis Pigmentosa – a degenerative disease that usually leads to blindness![2] It's a genetic disease but we had no trace of it in our family. My heart broke for Rebecca. She was so very brave, and not once did I hear complain or blame God.

It was the year her dream of running in the Olympics was shattered. She had continued training at a competitive level for years with injuries, running through them, but now was medically advised to stop running. Rebecca was so strong and, through the tears and over time she said,

God has a different race for me. All that I have learned as an athlete I can apply spiritually!

I learned so much from my daughter about selflessness!

It was the year our adored chocolate Labrador, Charlie Brown, died. Rebecca, Ben and Alex had grown up with him.

It was the year she parted ways with her University boyfriend.

But, the darkest hour came on November 8th 2005, when our precious Alex, took his life. The enemy of his soul had brought confusion to his mind and, while under the influence of a drug, he became delusional!

---

[2]   Rebecca had a very slow form of RP and her doctor was very hopeful for a cure – a big answer to our prayers.

Our Alex had a wonderful heart for people to come to faith in Christ, and this was the catalyst for Rebecca to relinquish all in honor of her brother's heart for the lost.

In a heart-shaped journal entry, I found Rebecca's words, *I've cried in the past over many things but never did I imagine it would be my baby brother, Alex, who would break my heart. We were planning Alex's 18th birthday party, not a funeral!*

From this deep place of anguish, Rebecca surrendered her broken heart to God.

She wrote,
I don't know what tomorrow holds but I know who holds me!

The one who believes in me will live, even though they die, and whoever lives by believing in me will never die. (John 11:25-26)

Our Heartfelt Prayer

Those who hope in the Lord will renew their strength. They will soar on wings like eagles; they will run and not grow weary, they will walk and not be faint. (Isaiah 40:31)

At Alex's memorial, Rebecca chose to read Isaiah 40, and our prayer is that this devotional will inspire you, and as you wait on the Lord, may He strengthen you and cause you to soar high on wings like an eagle.

May you run and not grow weary and may your sweet walk with Jesus revive and inspire others to hunger after God and to give their hearts to Christ. May the seeds sown by Rebecca and watered by our love and tears, bear much fruit through your life for God's glory and honor.

Honestly, I'm humbled that you even have this devotional in your hands. Rebeca stood once as we do, and would so very often tell me with all her heart, Mom! "Keep your eyes on Jesus, His perfect love casts out fear." I know, if it was right, very gently she would invite you to give your heart to Jesus, because she would always say, "tomorrow might be too late!"

Going Home

After we prayed, Rebecca hugged me one more time. Through the tears, I watched her as long as I could and, before she disappeared through the airport doors, she turned and gave me her beautiful Rebecca smile. And then she was gone!

I thanked the Lord for all he was doing in her life and for her sweet and courageous walk with Jesus. But, I never imagined that would be the last time on Earth I would see my beautiful daughter Rebecca.

Rebecca had returned from her speaking engagements in California, while we were in the UK visiting our precious son Ben, our sweet mums and attending an Alpha conference.

On the morning of May 8th 2014, she wentout for her routine run. It was a particularly hot day and Rebecca stopped by Lake Michigan to cool off. She had blood sugar issues and, tragically, we believe she probably fainted and fell into the water. Unable to get out where she had fallen in and due to the strong current, she tried to swim round to a boat ramp. This would have been easy for Rebecca but, with the water only just above freezing, after a brutal winter, our precious beautiful daughter was overcome by Hypothermia and drowned!! After seeing her call for help, four witnesses called 911, but they were too late!

There are no words to describe the pain and suffering in hearing the unimaginable, unbelievable, unthinkable news!!

After Alex went home, we watched Rebecca glorify God in her life, never imagining they would be her last 8 years on earth. Rebecca persevered in the race that God had set before her, faithfully continuing in her own rhythm, keeping her eyes on Jesus. She passed the finish line and, falling into His arms, she received her crown and joined Alex and others and went in to her tomorrow.

Birthing Awakening to God Ministries

After our precious Alex and Rebecca went home to Heaven, from the depths of our broken hearts and through overwhelming loud cries and tears, God birthed in Gerard and me a vision of His glory and His eternal plan and purpose.

Rebecca and Alex both went home on the 8th of the month, 8 years apart and they were both champion 800m runners. The number 8 in Hebrew means: 'New Beginnings!' and, independently, God gave Gerard and me the following scripture.

See, I am doing a new thing! Now it springs up; do you not perceive it? I am making a way in the wilderness and streams in the wasteland. (Isaiah 43:18-19)

We believe that nothing is wasted in God's Kingdom. He takes what the evil one intended to use to destroy us, and turns it around for His glory.

With the grace, love and comfort God gave us, we sensed Him calling us to share a message of love, comfort and hope to other broken and hurting hearts.

We are blessed beyond measure to have some wonderful brothers and sisters who stepped into our grief with us, and they generously helped us to birth, Awakening to God Ministries (ATG), with the founding scripture:

The Spirit of the Sovereign Lord is on me, because the Lord has anointed me to proclaim good news to the poor. He has sent me to bind up the brokenhearted, to proclaim freedom for the captives and release from darkness for the prisoners. (Isaiah 61:1)

When we view our suffering in the context of eternity, it takes on a new perspective.

Because of the joy awaiting Him, He (Jesus) endured the cross. (Hebrews 12:2, NLT)

ATG's logo is

8 on its side, means infinity.

Our big prayer is that God will visit us with another mighty "Awakening." Like a huge wave, we cry out for an "Awakening to God" to sweep around the world, bringing the knowledge of God's love to 2 billion people – a billion for each of our children. Rebecca wrote in her journal, *Ride the wave.*

How was Running from the Heart Birthed?

At the same time as finding Rebecca's journals, Lani, a dear friend of Rebecca, encouraged us with the words, "Rebecca's legacy must live on." This was then confirmed by several other dear friends.

Through prayer and many tears, we felt the best legacy we can give to our precious Rebecca, is to pass on her sweet walk with Jesus through the words found in her journals. However, my grief was debilitating and, finding it near impossible to read her journals, it took me a long time to start. I am thankful to God for the many dear friends who helped me to birth, *Running from the Heart*. I could not have done this alone.

Rebecca was an athlete and our heart-felt choice for the title, Running from the Heart, reflects her beautiful, unique and profound life.

Spending Time with God

The most important thing is my relationship with God.

In the morning, Rebecca would grab a cup of green tea and go to her comfy chair or favorite place with her Bible and journal. As in training, Rebecca was intentional about spending time with God. Preferably in the morning, but it is up to you. Train yourself to be Godly. Godliness is useful in every respect, both for now and the life to come. Training is the requirement of anything worth doing from studying to running to the Christian lifestyle. There are no shortcuts.

Exercise daily in God – no spiritual flabbiness, please! (1 Timothy 4:8 MSG)

Rebecca would encourage her soul with a thankful heart, her favorite worship songs, repentance, scripture and simply talking with God (prayer). When we meet with God, the Holy Spirit fills our hearts with love and He raises us up to be more than we can be.

We are sojourners. We are on a journey, which becomes spiritual when we encounter God. When we give our hearts to Him, our journey will take us to the true country, our true home.

The thing of first importance to Rebecca was her time with God. This was no casual Saturday afternoon run. She ran to God because her life depended on Him. She held tightly to the message of faith that Christ died for her sins, that Jesus was raised from the dead and that one day she would go to Heaven and not to Hell. This is what she rested on and believed until her very last breath.

Rebecca recognized the priorities, pressures and noise competing for her time with God but she trained herself to put God first.

How to read the Devotional

Throughout the devotional, I refer to Rebecca being home, because I believe Heaven is our true home.

As you read each devotional, start by slowly reading the bible verse and meditate on God's word. This will encourage and strengthen your heart. In a hand writing font are Rebecca's own journal entries, illustrating stories of her life, including her struggles and her joys, to which I've added my own thoughts.

And then I've included a very important part of Rebecca's time with God — Selah.

Why Selah?

Rebecca shared with me the importance and meaning of what Selah meant to her and it is written throughout her journals. It means to pause, think calmly and receive divine guidance. You have to create the time to listen to God.

Be still and know that I am God. (Psalm 46:10)

Stop, rest and wait, to reflect on who God says He is, in His word. We believe we see the world around us and yet it is only the surface that we perceive. We must learn the true nature of God in the world. Stop and rest, to keep things in perspective. Find balance between resting and working. To write down Gods blessings is a form of worship, as is having a thankful heart.

Rebecca learned solitude and silence in resting in His presence. She learned to block out the noise of the world. I think she called it blocking out the white noise (meaningless noise that takes our attention).

Passing the Baton: If I may, at the end of each devotional, I'd like to encourage you as a strong woman of faith, to take the baton and run with all your heart the race that God has planned for you. Make these a declaration before God, of how you are going to run your race.

Rebecca didn't do anything without prayer and each devotional ends with a prayer. Learn to breathe with slow prayers, praying about anything in your heart.

My prayer is that in the deep deepest place of your heart, you will deeply know the love, wonder, mystery, peace and the joy of meeting with God. May you have a life changing encounter with God, the maker of Heaven and Earth.

Jeannie Long

Rebecca's Prayer

My Father, you see all things. You Know
the beginning from the end. You are
the Alpha and Omega. You are love,
yet I have felt pain. You are present,
yet I have felt alone. You are joy, yet
I have felt a deep sadness. You are
light, yet I have only darkness. Still
I will trust you. My God your plan is
higher than mine and your thoughts
than mine. Use my grief for your glory.
May what the devil intended for evil
be used in a mighty way for good. May
you turn this night into day. God I
Know I am the apple of your eye. You
have protected my life when wicked
people were around me. You have
watched over my coming and going.
You have protected my life. You have
led me each step of the way.
God you are my Rock. You have
been my constant friend.
Amen.

Choose to Believe

Choose for yourself this day whom you will serve.
(Joshua 24:15)

I was moved to tears on finding this covenant in Rebecca's journal,
I choose to believe. I choose to trust. I choose to love. I choose the everlasting life you purchased for me on the cross. I choose your plan. I choose the pure love of Jesus Christ.

My Rebecca chose to give her heart to Jesus as a sweet young girl. She grew up in the church as a pastor's kid but was very honest about the questions she had about her faith. After much soul searching, she chose to believe the historic and other evidence that Jesus died on the cross and rose again. She chose to believe that He had died on the cross for her sins.

Experiencing God's love being poured into her heart by the Holy Spirit, Rebecca believed that Jesus Christ was not only her Savior but also the Lord of her life.

I'm so thankful to see you have called me to be your daughter and friend, please help me to put that love into practice – that your love, truth and salvation message are all reflected in how I live. Help me to bring that love whereever I go. Please can I be someone your Holy Spirit rests on and in.

My prayers were answered when Rebecca chose to ask Jesus into her heart. I choose to believe that Rebecca was called home because her life and work on earth were complete. In my mother's heart, it seems far too soon at 32, but I choose to believe it was God's perfect time. You see, Rebecca is not lost because she chose to believe that Jesus Christ was her Savior and I will see her and Alex again!

How true are Rebecca's words?
I don't know what tomorrow holds, I just know God holds me.

Selah

We love because he first loved us. (1 John 4:19)

We love Him because He first loved us and, His perfect love will cast all fear from your heart. Of all the people and things, you love on earth, it is your love for Jesus that will carry you through life.

"For you see, in the end, it is between you and God." Mother Theresa

I am humbled that you are reading this devotional. It is my prayer and, I truly believe, God is calling you today to choose to give your heart to Jesus Christ. If this is true for you, pray this prayer:

Lord Jesus, please forgive me, I'm sorry for all the wrong things I've done. I ask you to come into my heart and I choose to believe and to receive the everlasting life you purchased for me on the cross. Please fill my heart with your pure love, to follow you. Amen.

P.S. Tell someone!

If you are following Jesus, is there a part of your life that you need to surrender to Him?

Passing the Baton: Choose to believe and to trust God with your life.

Prayer: Dear Heavenly Father, thank you for the love you have poured into my heart by your Holy Spirit. Please help me and strengthen my heart with your grace to believe, to surrender all to you and to trust you with my life. Amen.

Faith to Persevere

And let us run with perseverance the race marked out for us; fixing our eyes on Jesus, the pioneer and perfecter of faith. (Hebrews 12:1-2)

What happens to your faith when you suffer? Rebecca was suffering from a broken heart.

Never did I think in a million years that it would be my brother, Alex, who would break my heart. I feel deeply for my parents, my brother Ben, and for the people who feel sad for us.

Rebecca poured out the ache of her broken heart onto the pages on her journal. She grieved and mourned deeply the unexpected death of her youngest brother Alex. Not just any death, but a suicide! It dramatically changed the course of her life. Rebecca continued on her journey of faith with many questions.

Where were you God? Why didn't you help my brother? I just want my brother back and my family back to how it was! How can I put my faith in you now?

She wrote of her faith being challenged to the depths and wavered back and forth between lament and trust. In the struggle, the athlete in Rebecca knew how to exercise her faith muscles. She ran to God in prayer and found solace in His presence. In that intimate place, she gave her broken heart over to her heavenly Father. She wrote,

You are the author of my story and perfecter of my faith....if you've allowed my heart to be broken, it must be for an even greater eternal purpose.

Instead of growing bitter and hardened by her debilitating circumstances, she accepted the race marked out for her. She chose to let the Lord's sweetness flow from her broken heart; in God's providence, they were the last eight years of her life on Earth.

Selah

Trust in the LORD with all your heart and lean not on your own understanding; in all your ways submit to Him, and He will make your paths straight. (Proverbs 3:5-6)

Your days may not always go as you hope, but in whatever you are facing, know that God wants you to call on Him and to draw you near to His heart. Train yourself like the athlete. Develop your faith muscles to be fighting fit and run with perseverance the race that God has planned for you.

What can you do today to strengthen your faith muscles to persevere?

Passing the Baton: Accept the race that God has marked out for you. Do not allow your heart to become bitter but keep yourself in God's love. Ask God to help you to know the comforting love and gentle whispers of the

Holy Spirit. Whatever your faith is up against, learn to run freely in God's love and call on your life.

Rebecca's Prayer: *Oh Heavenly Father, I don't understand? But I thank you that you are the Author and the Perfecter of my faith. I ask for strength and courage and grace, to persevere, and I welcome you Holy Spirit to fill me afresh today with all that I need to sustain me. I take this leap of faith and offer up my broken heart. Amen.*

Faith to Persevere and Rebecca's Heart Cry weave together. Rebecca writes of her struggle of faith and, because of her perseverance, God graciously gave her an inspired moment, that shaped her heart cry for the rest of her life.

Rebecca's Heart Cry

You intended to harm me, but God intended it for good to accomplish what is now being done, the saving of many lives. (Genesis 50:20)

In a divine and inspired moment, God led Rebecca to Genesis 50:20. This verse became the cry of her heart and she lived the rest of her days for the "saving of many lives."

Rebecca's heart was broken when her brother, Alex, went home to Heaven at just seventeen years old. It was through this overwhelming suffering that she began to understand the depth of the suffering of God's heart when His son Jesus was dying on the cross for her sins, and the sins of the whole world. How could a loving God allow such suffering? As she mourned her brother, she agonized over this question, she wrote,

God sometimes allows us to go through great suffering for an even greater eternal purpose...

Faith is a gift from God and He who calls you is faithful to carry you through...

My job is to bring heaven to earth through my prayers and my obedience...

My life must be living in response to what my father is doing, not as a reaction against the darkness...

Her heart marked forever in memory of this divine moment, she wore a heart-shaped locket with a photo of Alex and Gen 50:20.

Every life is precious, I pray I can make a difference by sharing the love of Jesus.

Rebecca desperately missed her brother but, she found peace in knowing that he had given his heart to Jesus and was home in heaven.

Rebecca had always had a heart for the "Lost," but after Alex went home, she humbly laid her life down, her heart now consumed at the very thought of a young person dying before ever knowing of God's love for them in Jesus Christ.

Don't put off helping someone today because they might not have tomorrow.

Her prayers were answered when God opened the door for her to become the USA Director for Alpha Youth (Alpha is a course to introduce people to Jesus Christ).

Rebecca relinquished everything to see the purpose of God in her generation.

Selah

For God so loved the world that He gave His one and only Son, that whoever believes in Him shall not perish but have eternal life. (John 3:16)

Suffering is a mystery! Sometimes grief and tears are all we have as we embrace the pain. Allow God to hold you at this time and he will bring healing to your heart. God is close to the broken hearted.

Grieve your loss to the point of relinquishing all to Him and He will turn it for good to bring glory to His name.

God has the eternal perspective and one day you will too.

Passing the Baton: Do you declare to love the Lord your God with all your heart and soul, to make him Lord of your time, investing your days wisely for Kingdom work? Do you believe this is a day to run for Jesus, that the harvest is ready and that God will never abandon you? Do you want to live like that in full abandon?

Rebecca's Prayer: *Dear Heavenly Father, please use my grief for your glory. May what the devil intended for evil be used in a mighty way for good. May you turn this dark night into a bright new day. Amen.*

A Christian Lifestyle

We are Christ's ambassadors; God is making his appeal through us. We speak for Christ when we plead, "Come back to God!" (2 Corinthians 5:20, NLT)

I felt God speak to me on a run. He told me that as a Shepherd, He was gathering His sheep from across the world.

Rebecca was humbled to be invited to write an article for a Christian magazine, in which she described what a Christian lifestyle looked like. The following are a few excerpts:

We are Christ's ambassadors for the lost souls in this broken world. We are His eyes, ears, feet and voice. It requires building a close relationship with God, so His Spirit can work through us and draw people to Jesus. Being a witness of God's love is a lifestyle. It's about sharing Christ's love by building relationships and creating opportunities for God's Spirit to touch other people's hearts.

Rebecca went on to explain in more detail how to live the Christian lifestyle.

Jesus said, "As the Father has sent Me, I am sending you." Spend a lot of time praying for your friends and family (we found lists of people she was praying for in her journal). *Through prayer, seek God's heart, wisdom and direction, for our battle takes place in the Heavenly realm. Be intentional about going into the community and building relationships. Listen and respect others, even if you disagree. Never judge but always love. Our job is to bring Jesus' love into others' lives, simply doing life and showing interest in others is an important step to allowing God's Spirit to work through us.*

Dress in the wardrobe God picked out for you: compassion, kindness, humility, quiet strength... And regardless of what else you put on, wear love. (Colossians 3:12 and 14, The Message)

A friend wrote the following kind words, which reflect the heart of hundreds of messages received after Rebecca went home.

"Rebecca's beautiful life was poured out as a sweet fragrance for Jesus... She had a contagious smile and a willingness to listen as others spoke. She was a beautiful flower of grace falling on all those around her and those yet to come through her life story."

Selah

You will receive power when the Holy Spirit comes on you; and you will be my witnesses. (Acts 1:8)

Be an ambassador extraordinaire. It is not the length of days that profit you, but the days in His service, bringing glory to God. Go out into your community; be amazingly creative in how you share God's love to the world. It is

God's will! And, remember, God has promised to equip you with power, through the Holy Spirit, to be a witness for Him.

How can you share God's love and make a difference for the people that God has placed in your life?

Passing the Baton: Live a lifestyle that attracts people to Jesus. Beautiful are those who bring the "Good News."

Prayer: Heavenly Father, please give me your heart for the people you have and will bring into in my life. Help me to remember that I am your eyes, ears, hands and voice on Earth. Please help me to be your ambassador, sharing your love and kindness revealed in Jesus Christ. Amen.

The Hope of Seeing Beyond

Those who hope in the LORD will renew their strength.
They will soar on wings like eagles; they will run and not
grow weary; they will walk and not be faint. (Isaiah 40:31)

God showed me Isaiah 40:28-31 on the day my
17-year-old brother Alex took his life, in 2005.

Rebecca was so brave when she spoke at her brother's memorial service and, although faint with sorrow, I remember her sweet voice reading Isaiah 40:28-31. After the service, there was a profound moment, that gave me a glimmer of hope in the Lord, when several people shared they had seen an eagle circling the church.

Living in the tension of her broken heart, Rebecca sensed the hope of the resurrection like never before. In her journals, I found this letter that didn't get sent but, in a way it has, because you are kindly reading it!

I feel Isaiah 40:28-31 are from God to you, and
offer you great HOPE. Hope is your firm assurance
regarding things in your life that are unclear and
unknown. No matter what you're facing or have
faced, put your hope in the Lord and, I know, He
will give you more strength.

God sent Christ to die for us and if we only ask,
He will be with us for life. I can truly say at this
time that nothing in this life (not fame or wealth

or any other gratification) will ever compare to knowing and having a relationship with God.

Jesus Christ is the only hope for this broken world. There is nothing else worth living for than to see Him glorified and His name lifted high in all the Earth. His resurrection from the dead gives us great hope for the life to come. Christ in you is the hope of glory!

I hope and pray that these words will bring hope to your heart.

As she waited on the Lord, her strength was renewed and she felt a calling to start a hand painted card and letter writing ministry, to bring hope and comfort to siblings who were suffering like herself.

Selah

May the God of hope fill you with all joy and peace as you trust in him, so that you may overflow with hope by the power of the Holy Spirit. (Romans 15:13)

Whatever you're facing, God wants you to share with Him the cry of your heart. As you chose to put your trust in Him, He will strengthen you with His whispers of hope for a better tomorrow. Encourage yourself with God's promises, they are an anchor for your soul.

What does it mean to you, to trust God for your future? How can God use you to bring hope to others?

Passing the Baton: As you trust in Him, be filled with joy and peace and overflow with hope by the power of the Holy Spirit.

Prayer: Dear Jesus! My hope comes from you; truly you are my rock and my salvation. Thank you for the power of your Holy Spirit to fill my heart with joy and peace as I trust in you. Thank you for helping me and strengthening me when I am weak. You are not only my friend who helps me, but you are my only hope. Amen.

Rebecca's Dream

God can tell you what it means and set you at ease.
(Genesis 41:16, NLT)

The verse above refers to a dream that Pharaoh had about the future, which came true. God uses dreams throughout the Bible to speak to His people.

Sometimes God can speak to us through our dreams today.

In our darkest hours, we received an invitation from our dear friends, who not only opened their hearts to our overwhelming grief, but also invited us to their peaceful home in Mexico.

Watching a beautiful sunset, Rebecca's brother Ben pointed out seven wild horses walking in a line along the golden beach. It took my breath away because I sensed it had something to do with Rebecca and not just because she loved horses.

On returning to the US, I read these words in one of Rebecca's journals.

I dreamt last night that I owned a horse I loved, and in my dream, I was riding my horse with about seven others and I was the last one in the line.

Through the power of the resurrection of Jesus Christ and in His providence, I sensed God comforting me that

Rebecca is safely home with Him and her brother Alex! A friend later shared her own dream of Rebecca riding a horse in heaven! I am undone!

Selah

I am the resurrection and the life. Anyone who believes in me will live even after dying. Everyone who lives in me and believes in me will never ever die. Do you believe this? (John 11:25-26, NLT)

Every so often, God gives us a glimpse of the bigger picture. Yes! it's a mystery, but our mysteries are miraculously answered in the unmatched name of Jesus.

Do you fear death and, if so, what conclusion have you reached in light of the scriptures above?

Passing the Baton: Keep your heart open to God's voice.

Prayer: Dear Heavenly Father, thank you that my life with you will go on forever. Thank you that the source of all joy is being in your presence both now and always. Amen.

Joy

The joy of the Lord is your strength. (Nehemiah 8:10)

I choose my savior Jesus Christ. He is the author and perfecter of my faith. I pray that I might drink the cup that God has assigned me with joy- the joy of the Lord is my strength...

Like warming up before a race, Rebecca knew how critical it was to spend time with Jesus before the start of her day. The Lord was the source of her joy, even when her soul was downcast.

Through reading her Bible, worship and thanksgiving she encouraged her soul and found His joy.

Rebecca's journals reflect the joy that flows from sweet fellowship with Jesus Christ.

Joy is the fruit of being loved by God. And, from being rooted in His gracious love, joy flows.

I'm here to show His glory in my life. Joy, peace and love take their place in my heart, I am thankful and eternally grateful for this, for I see Jesus himself is my JOY.

Even in the midst of heartbreak, Rebecca experienced moments of joy that she knew to be a gift from God. It is often in times of great trials that you can feel angry and abandoned by God, but even in her darkest times, Rebecca chose to stay true to her Father in Heaven.

On a mother daughter shopping outing, while Rebecca was picking out a gift for a friend, I found myself rather taken by a basket full of polished shiny stones. Each one had an inspiring word engraved into it. I asked Rebecca to choose a stone that could be my gift to her. Rebecca chose Joy!

It took my breath away because we had all been very tearful that morning, missing our Alex. I could not believe she would choose joy above everything else. Like many times before, I saw she was a willing, broken vessel. She allowed Jesus to pour His wisdom and grace gently through to me. Her beautiful eyes and smile said it all; she was encouraging me to choose joy as well.

Selah

You will fill me with joy in your presence. (Psalm 16:11)

Jesus Christ is the source of all joy. You may know happiness for a time from the circumstances in your life, but this is far different from the joy that is a spiritual gift and comes from the Holy Spirit.

The joy that God gives is available in His presence, even in the midst of pain, sorrow and grief. In choosing joy you will glorify God by revealing the beauty of Jesus Christ in your life. Others will have a glimpse into your life and wonder, *how do they live so joyfully and gracefully even in the face of great suffering?* You can be a walking testament to the healing and restoring power of Jesus Christ.

How well do you know, "The joy of the Lord is your strength?"

Passing the Baton: Choose joy today

Prayer: Dear Heavenly Father, thank you for the gift of joy. Please help me to glorify Jesus by choosing joy no matter the circumstances. Amen.

While writing this devotional, I came across an old birthday card to me from Rebecca and the verse was, *The Joy of the Lord is your Strength.* (Nehemiah 8:10)

Disciplined Thinking

Fix your thoughts on what is true, and honorable, and right, and pure, and lovely, and admirable. Think about things that are excellent and worthy of praise. (Philippians 4:8, NLT)

Keep your eyes focused on what is right and look straight ahead to what is good. Pay attention to God's word and don't ever forget His word. Keep it always in your mind. This is the Key to life.
Be careful what you think about because your thoughts run your life.

In the dark days after Alex went home, I searched for God but my thinking was very confused. Although Rebecca was grieving herself, I remember the sweetness of her love and the comfort of her words and prayers, as we wept together. She encouraged me to fix my thoughts on God's promises and the hope we have for the future, reminding me to see the bigger picture and often saying;

"I wonder what Alex is doing now?"

Her words of truth touched my aching heart in a profound way and somewhere in my soul, deep was calling to deep, bringing a glimmer of hope. Yes! "What was my Alex doing?"

Rebecca always encouraged me to keep moving through the grieving process. Later, I could almost hear her voice, as I found written in her journal,

Keep focused on the step in front of you, the process hurts so much but nothing else matters... Keep moving.

As an athlete, Rebecca learned how important it was to keep her mind focused on her race, especially when the going was tough and negative thoughts could hinder her.

You don't have to be an athlete to feel pain. In the storms of life, you may well feel pain and your thinking becomes confused.

In the storms of her life, Rebecca held on to the promises of God. She trusted God's word to the very core of her being and with her whole heart she worshipped the God of her salvation, as she fixed her thoughts on what is true and worthy of praise.

I am thankful for creation and beauty — they give me a vision to see and think about things with a fresh new perspective.

Selah

Do not conform to the pattern of this world, but be transformed by the renewing of your mind. (Romans 12:2)

Train yourself to be disciplined in your thinking. Don't let your thoughts run wild but believe the truth of God's word every day of your life. Renew your mind with the word of God, hold fast to what is true, resist the lies of the devil and he will flee from you. So, run with all your heart for the best is yet to come.

What negative thought patterns do you need to change today?

Passing the Baton: Be intentional, hold fast to what is true and resist all negative thoughts. Think about whatever is pure and lovely and beautiful and praiseworthy...

Prayer: My Heavenly Father, I humbly ask you to help me to discipline my mind to resist the negative thoughts. Please open my eyes that I may see more of you in your word and your creation. I want my thoughts to be focused on you. Amen.

Rebecca's Prayer: *Dear Heavenly Father, my feelings scream out that I'm unworthy, Oh God! please give me a disciplined mind to refuse these lies and give me wisdom, give me everything. When I look into myself I am so weak, but I choose to keep looking at God's face. I need more of God's Holy Spirit to strengthen me. Amen.*

Wisdom

Teach us to number our days, that we may gain a heart of wisdom. (Psalm 90:12)

Today I have been thinking about the opportunities God gives us to glorify Him in both the good and the bad things. Everything has meaning deeper than I understand now.

The pain of Alex going home early has pulled me into the urgency of the moment. I want to give my life for something that will last forever. Please show me what to do, where to go and what to say.

At the start of each new day, she ran to the heart of God. Her priority was,

To love Him first and foremost. To put Him first above anything else.

Rebecca prayed each day for wisdom and understanding to make the most of every opportunity.

No one knows when our time is up, and Alex going home shocked Rebecca into the realities of Heaven. It took her to a deep place of understanding her days in the context of eternity. It pushed her to understand the eternal value of her decisions.

For the Son of Man is going to come in His Father's glory with His angels, and then He will reward each person according to what they have done. (Matthew 16:27)

We all live for something. But it is not wisdom if that something is not God. Wisdom teaches us that our life is a mist, and every breath that we breathe should be to please God.

The first way to please God is to love Him with all your heart, with all your soul and with all your strength. This is wisdom.

When bad things happen, we might feel like running away, but Rebecca learned that through these times, the wise thing to do is to run to God.

God has our days numbered... they are His, God is sovereign. The Key is to trust God.

Selah

Every day of my life was recorded in your book. Every moment was laid out before a single day had passed. (Psalm 139:16, NLT)

Each day is a gift from God and may hold a surprise. Don't be afraid to face the uncertainties of each day. Whether happy or sad, know that God is merciful, redemptive and does not make mistakes. He is your past, He is your future and He is with you today. Develop a wise heart by keeping the first priority first and steward your time, your gifts and your opportunities for the glory of God.

Check your priorities – are they helping you to steward the things God has placed in your hands today?

Passing the Baton: Embrace the eternal importance of your decisions.

Prayer: Dear Heavenly Father, teach me your wisdom today in how to live to bring glory to your name. Thank you that this day is already written in your book, and please help me to choose to walk today in all the things you have prepared for me. Amen.

The Holy Spirit

And I will pray the Father, and He will give you another Helper, that He may abide with you forever the Spirit of truth, whom the world cannot receive, because it neither sees Him nor knows Him; but you know Him, for He dwells with you and will be in you. (John 14:16-17, NKJV)

Dear Father, can I please be someone that your Holy Spirit rests on and in. As I carry God's Holy Spirit, you are my strength, I am not alone, you are my helper, and you are with me and for me. I ask that you help me to be led by your Spirit and not by my flesh. Amen.

A precious gift is the presence of the Holy Spirit in our life. He is a sweet and rich and deep treasure.

Through her life, Rebecca learned more and more to live a life that depended on the Holy Spirit to guide and help her on the path God planned for her. Her heart leaned on and trusted Him.

God's love has been poured out into our hearts through the Holy Spirit. Please help me to put your love into practice, that your love, truth and salvation message are all reflected in how I live. Not letting lesser things rob, of the most important love relationship.

The fruit of the Holy Spirit is love, joy, peace, patience, kindness, goodness, faithfulness, gentleness and self-control. I want all of these!

"I want all of these," touched my heart because this was a true expression of how Rebecca lived out her faith in what were to be the last years of her life. She was desperate for God's presence in her life and was sensitive to avoid grieving the Holy Spirit in thought, word or action.

Thank you that you are teaching me to glide with you on the wings of your Spirit. We will tell the next generation the praiseworthy deeds of the Lord.

Selah

You will receive power when the Holy Spirit comes on you; and you will be my witnesses. (Acts 1:8)

Your body is the temple of the Holy Spirit. (1 Corinthians 6:19)

The most important relationship in your life is with God. God never intended that you try and follow Jesus on your own – there is too much against you. When you received Jesus Christ as your Lord and Savior, the Holy Spirit came to live in your heart. He will guide you and give you the strength to follow Christ and be a witness for Him. He will also convict you of sin and of the things you should do to please God.

Be filled with the Holy Spirit. Ephesians 5:18 means we can regularly ask God to fill us afresh with the Holy Spirit.

What are the things that are stopping you from asking the Holy Spirit to fill you afresh today?

Passing the Baton: Pray for God's help, and more help, to be desperate for God's presence in your life.

Prayer: Dear Heavenly Father, please fill me with your Holy Spirit today that I may love what you love and do what you would do. Breathe on me, breath of God; until I am totally yielded to you, until this Earthly part of me glows with your divine fire, until this life that I now live is not mine but yours. In Jesus name, I come to you in prayer and worship. Amen.

(Adapted from the hymn, "Breathe on me breath of God," by Edwin Hatch)

Travel Light

Let us throw off everything that hinders and the sin that so easily entangles. And let us run with perseverance the race marked out for us. (Hebrews 12:1)

This is our time to show the world who Jesus Christ is, to be His hands and feet, to shine light and bring hope and healing to the world... Running a great race-finish with great faith!

You're here to be light, bringing out the God colors in the world. God is not a secret to be kept.

It should be a natural outflowing of our walk/ relationship with God. Travel light to be a traveling light.

Rebecca learned how to throw off everything that might hinder people from seeing the light of Jesus in her life.

In this season God has been teaching me to:

- Leave behind fear and have a fresh perspective of God's love for me;
- Give Him my worries and to trust Him with all my heart;
- Throw off discouragement and persevere in the race God has set for me;

- *Take every impure thought captive, live a pure life set apart for God – Jesus is coming for a spotless bride;*
- *Guard against prideful thoughts that can creep in, I ask God to keep me humble each day; and*
- *Forgive as Jesus has forgiven me.*

A few of many kind words received about our precious Rebecca.

"It was as if we could all see an angelic halo around her – how she lived spoke volumes about her faith."

Selah

You are the light of the world... Let your light shine before others, that they may see your good deeds and glorify your Father in Heaven. (Matthew 5:14, 16)

Watch out for the light-dimming, love quenching thoughts and actions that weigh you down and prevent you from shining brightly for the glory of God. Throw off the hindrances and the sins that can so easily entangle and distract you from God's plan for your life.

Think of your life as a journey to Heaven – what are you carrying that is weighing you down?

Passing the Baton: Travel light; be a travelling light.

Prayer: Dear Heavenly Father, please help me to travel light by throwing off the things that quench your love and dim your light within me. Father, please help me to share your love and light with those who are in darkness and in need. Amen.

Unique

I praise you because I am fearfully and wonderfully made; your works are wonderful, I know that full well. (Psalm 139:14)

How do I see creation? God speaks through everything he has made...

Today Beautiful, large snowflakes fall slowly, softly, and peacefully to the ground. Each one unique...

In that quiet and reflective place, Rebecca heard the gentle whisper of the Holy Spirit.

I am also God's workmanship. He created me, He loves me and approves of me. He loves me unconditionally and wholeheartedly and continually. God speaks through everything he has made.

I am His masterpiece, with a unique call!

Rebecca responded to God's call on her life. She understood and trusted that through the circumstances of her life, God was preparing and training her to live out her calling.

There is peace in my heart. Everything has been for my good to soften my heart for what God has created me to do.

God's work and calling on everyone's life is unique and, because of this, it makes no sense to compare oneself with anyone else. No two snowflakes are alike, and neither are we. Rebecca wrote,

I can never live someone else's life, only mine.

The beauty of the Lord was upon Rebecca in many ways, and she was humbled to see and use the gifts that God had given her. Writing,

God, in your calling on my life, help me accept the things I cannot change and give me courage to change the things I can.

Although she often felt inadequate, Rebecca had a gift to speak in public. God graciously opened the door for invitations to share across the US and around the world. She spoke courageously about Jesus and she brought comfort and encouragement, especially challenging the youth to give their hearts and to run for Jesus.

Selah

Your eyes saw my unformed body; all the days ordained for me were written in your book before one of them came to be. (Psalm 139:16)

God created each us for a specific time and purpose and none of us know when the days ordained for us will end. Be open to the guidance of the Holy Spirit until your unique calling becomes the most important thing in your life. Your legacy will have an impact for those who come after you.

What is holding you back from finding and living for God's unique call on your life?

Passing the Baton: Be thankful for the unique gifts that God has given to you and, by His grace, use them with wisdom and courage.

Prayer: Dear Heavenly Father, thank you for creating me, for making me unique and for loving me just as I am. Please lead me to find the special purpose you have for my life and help me to be content in living to please you. Amen.

Friendship

A friend loves at all times. (Proverbs 17:17)

My friends and family are precious to me, I am thankful and eternally grateful for them...
When my friends meet me, I want them to meet Jesus! I see that my friends are a gift from God and loving them is a form of worship unto the Lord.

Rebecca loved her friends! The lovely thing about her friendships was that they were not just about her but about allowing the Holy Spirit to touch people through her. Judging by the hundreds of letters received after she went home, her friends were inspired and encouraged by their sweet friendship with Rebecca.

"Rebecca's faith, kindness and strength, in the midst of her own grief, impressed me so much that I renewed my faith."

"Not many people have the talent to make you feel that you are more important to them than themselves. Rebecca had it! It made my day when I saw her. Thank you, Lord, for the gift of Rebecca's friendship."

"The best friend... the best sister... your beautiful smile... loyal and kind to everyone you met... your strength of faith we admired so much... you would light up a room and fill it with grace... your contagious laughter, beautiful face and sincere embrace.... Teaching, inspiring with the lightest of touch..."

It moved me to tears to find lists of friends and family in her journals that were loved and prayed for! Rebecca was a very loyal friend.

Selah

Greater love has no one than this: to lay down one's life for one's friends. You are my friends if you do what I command. (John 15:13-14)

The Holy Spirit working in your life will guide you in how to become a loyal and faithful friend.

If you have never met Jesus Christ and would like to have a relationship with the perfect friend, as your Savior, I invite you to say this prayer to invite Him into your heart:

Lord Jesus, please forgive me, have mercy on me, I'm sorry for all the wrong things I have done. I ask you to come into my heart and I choose to believe and to receive the everlasting life you purchased for me on the cross. Please fill my heart with your pure love, to follow you. Amen.

P.S. This is a life-changing step. Tell someone!

If you do know Jesus as your friend, let your sweet friendships be a fragrant offering unto Him. You are truly blessed to be a blessing.

What would you like your friends to say about you?

Passing the Baton: When your friends meet you, may they meet Jesus.

Prayer: Pray for 3 friends: Dear God, I pray for [insert your friend's name] and please give me a way to bless them today. Amen.

As I worked on this devotional, I received a phone call. The caller was missing Rebecca and shared how she would have liked, more than anything, to have chatted and prayed something over with her. My eyes filled with tears. What a legacy of love and friendship. I am undone!

Fall into His Arms

The eternal God is your refuge, and underneath are the everlasting arms. (Deuteronomy 33:27)

I just want to let go and fall into your arms. To hold me and carry me in the times when I'm weak. You are mighty to hold me. You are with me and for me. You are my helper.

Rebecca was on a bike ride with her friends through Manhattan when her brakes suddenly gave out. When the kind young man she was with, saw her struggling to keep control of her bike, he caught her in his arms, making a joke about her falling for him. Rebecca thanked the Lord she wasn't hurt and saw the funny side of it. On reflection, she felt God spoke to her heart that He was always there for her and that she was safe in His mercy and protection.

Rebecca wrote,

My life is in your hands and Lord I will trust you, you are sovereign. As we step forward, God is above us and beneath our feet, He has already prepared the way, God's love is so deep, it's beyond our comprehension. It wasn't until I surrendered my life, and received God's love, that I finally became free.

Rebecca would go to her favorite place each morning for quiet time with God. She would settle into her a cozy chair with her Bible, journal and a green tea, and seek God by reading His love letter to her and listening for His gentle whispers. She sensed the balm of Jesus' peace and His gift of grace to strengthen her for the day.

Selah

Don't be afraid, for I am with you. Don't be discouraged, for I am your God. I will strengthen you and help you. I will hold you up with my victorious right hand. (Isaiah 41:10, NLT)

In the midst of life's troubles, when you are feeling overwhelmed, remember that God holds everything together by the power of His word. Give to God your fears and allow the Holy Spirit to fill your heart with God's love and comfort. He will strengthen and guide you with every step and underneath you are His everlasting arms.

What is stopping you from resting in God's arms today? What are the worries or fears that you need to hand over to Him?

Passing the Baton: Trust God and give all fear and discouragement over to Him.

Prayer: Dear Heavenly Father, God of all comfort, thank you that no matter what I go through you are with me. Thank you for giving me your Holy Spirit to be my comforter and helper. I give to you my concern/s about [name exactly what it is and the feeling you have about the concern/s e.g. fear, guilt etc.] Thank you for holding me and supporting me. I trust in you with all my heart and not in my own understanding. Amen.

The Father's Love

See what great love the Father has lavished on us, that we should be called children of God! (1 John 3:1)

He loves you and approves of you. He may not approve of everything you do, but He loves you unconditionally, wholeheartedly and continuously.

Though I have not seen Him, my heart Knows Him. The Holy Spirit has revealed the Father's heart.

God is a good, good father all the time! I am thankful and blessed. It is an honor to have such a loving Heavenly Father who loves and trusts me.

I'm thankful and blessed for the many new things revealed to my heart. Everyone is valued, everyone is loved by their heavenly Father. I seem to be able to see things through my Father's eyes. As I look into their eyes I have compassion to see what they're going through and feel it with them. I want to be a source of hope when others can't find hope.

Rebecca was blessed to have an earthly father who loved and adored her and was always there for her.

Rebecca was the favorite to win the London 800m school's championship, but during the race a competitor pushed her to the ground. My heart missed a beat as she lay motionless on the track. In an instant, her Dad ran to help her. Lifting her up in his arms, she was rushed to hospital in an ambulance.

She had broken several ribs and was badly bruised but, even in her great pain, our sweet hearted Rebecca forgave the competitor. After recovering, she trained even harder and went on to become state champion.

We cherish the card that Rebecca hand painted as a thank you,

Thank you, Dad, for being my rock, and my hero, I'm proud to be your daughter.

Selah

Keep me as the apple of your eye. (Psalm 17:8)

The wonder of the Father's love for us is overwhelming. He has such an interest in each of us. His word reveals that our relationship with Him is the richest of all relationships. He loves you because He loves you and not for what you can do for Him.

The relationship with your earthly father may be difficult but you have a Father in Heaven who loves you unconditionally and has promised to never leave you. Let Him hold you and carry you through life.

In what ways have you experienced the pure love that your Heavenly Father has lavished on you?

Passing the Baton: Receive the gift of faith, and live in the truth of your Heavenly Father's perfect love for you.

Prayer: My dear Heavenly Father, thank you for your unconditional and everlasting love for me. Thank you that I am the apple of your eye and that you have forgiven my sins. Please help me to live in the truth of your love for me. I choose to trust and love you with all my heart. In Jesus' name. Amen.

Solitude

Be still and know I am God. (Psalm 46:10)

Celebrate the discipline of solitude.

Rebecca was always dipping into the book of Psalms and many of them are written out and underlined in her journals. Psalm 46:10 was one of her favorites and she practiced the discipline of solitude in order to be still and hear the divine whispers.

Rebecca had learned the difference between loneliness and solitude. The uncertainties of life had left her feeling vulnerable and through her grief she had times of loneliness, writing:

Noise and distractions can help for a while but in the end, you are still lonely...

It took courage to face the fear of loneliness but it was in these times that she found that she was not truly alone.

God is with me and will help me... I am not alone!

Rebecca learned that she could turn loneliness into solitude.

Solitude leads to peace whereas loneliness leads to anxiety. Solitude is enjoyable but loneliness is unpleasant.

She was learning not to rush in and out of God's presence; training herself to listen to the divine whispers through prayer and Bible study.

I am thankful for this season: "He who began a good work in me will carry it on to completion." He has pruned the areas of my heart that have been proud and deceived, misled, selfish etc. There is a new peace in my heart and it will keep growing, I understand the magnitude of the sacrifice that has been made for me. God has been speaking to me this whole time and I missed so much.

As an athlete, Rebecca would find a quiet place to be alone before a race. It was in the quietness that she thought through her tactics and gathered courage and strength for what was ahead.

Selah

Jesus often withdrew...for prayer. (Luke 5:16, NLT)

In the hustle and bustle, it's all too easy to get distracted with the worries and noise of life. The enemy of your soul wants to rob you from hearing the gentle divine whispers... God is always with you; give yourself times of quietness to receive His comfort, peace and strength.

What are the distractions that stop you from intentionally spending regular quiet time with the Lord?

Passing the Baton: Be intentional about spending regular time to be quiet with the Lord and to listen to the gentle divine whispers of the Holy Spirit.

Rebecca's prayer: Dear Lord, thank you that you teach me to come to you, to learn about being still, the secret of solitude. Thank you that you teach me that I don't have to strive or do anything in my strength. Please help me to take time to turn off the noise in my life and to come aside to receive the comfort and strength that only you can provide. Thank you that in quietness and trusting in you, there is great peace. Amen.

Purpose

For I know the plans I have for you, declares the Lord, plans to prosper you and not to harm you, plans to give you hope and a future. (Jeremiah 29:11)

I want to see the purpose of God in my generation and live my life for something that will last forever...

These powerful words were Rebecca's heart cry and she came to see that God's plans and purpose for her could only be learned through affliction and a broken heart.

I am seeing new things, perhaps the struggle, this illness, has helped me see things in a new way, and that is a positive outcome. I would never have understood the depths of purpose, if God had not brought me through the afflictions of my life. Bringing me to see the reality of surrendering my plans, seeing they are not always the best direction for me. That God is in control. Many things have happened that are out of my control, but through it all I see the purpose of God for my life through my broken heart. If God chose to break my heart I can thank him to bring His purpose through my broken heart.

In her affliction, Rebecca also learned that she could trust and rely on God's promises to strengthen and comfort her in the dark days.

In quietness and trust is my strength.

I thought I understood but in my weakness and brokenness I have learned that God is my strength and He is my hope.

Rebecca took her pain and questions to God and her prayers were full of faith as she trusted in the promise of God's word.

Dear Lord, thank you for your perfect plans, your perfect timing, your perfect promises. I trust you my God and savior... I want to follow you with my whole heart. Amen.

God's purpose and plans last forever and Rebecca wrote:

"He is no fool who gives what he cannot keep in order to gain what he cannot lose." Jim Elliot

Jim Elliot was 28 years old when he was called home - Rebecca grew up hearing this quote from her Dad, also one of her spiritual heroes.

Selah

In quietness and trust is your strength. (Isaiah 30:15)

God has a purpose and a plan for your life and shapes you through your life's journey. The family you were born into, your gifts, your experiences, the Bible, godly council and prayer are all ways the Lord guides you into His purpose and plan for your life. Quietness and trusting in

God is the key to your strength. He will give you all that you need for the race He has planned for you.

Whose plans are you going to follow – your own or God's? What is it that drives you?

Passing the Baton: With a confident step, **live** your life for something that will last forever.

Prayer: Dear God, thank you for the plans you have for me. Please fill me with the knowledge of your will and give me the courage to go your way and not the way of the world. Amen.

During the time of writing this devotional, Rebecca's dear friend, her husband and 2 boys, kindly came to visit and she mentioned she was reading, *The Purpose Driven Life*, of all the books! It moved me to tears. Rebecca was led to read this book back in 2004, during a time when she had a running injury. She encouraged everybody she knew at the time to read this book, including me.

Struggles

Fight the good fight of the faith. Take hold of the eternal life to which you were called... (1 Timothy 6:12)

I'm struggling! It's an excruciating moment to be faced with your own darkness. I take responsibility and repent for all the wrong I've done, my heart has broken for the hurt I have caused God, countless wrong choices, temptations. There is a lot I regret that I must and am handing over to God. The process continues...

I'm struggling with the areas of frustration that my "seeing" is limited. I realize this is a fight and want to honor God with my life, keep on trusting Him that He's got this. Trust is the key. I am thankful that God trusts me to reveal hidden treasures and gems in His time...

God, what is it you're asking me to do? I feel so inadequate at times and know such a small part of what you're doing. I TRUST YOU. I will choose to do my part — to focus, to focus on Jesus. To accept His love, to give His love, to honor the Lord...

God gives us each a cup we must drink and I cannot compare myself and will not compare myself with another. All I know is what I've seen and experienced and that has helped me better understand Christ's love for me and for every precious soul. Again, I am humbled. The victory is *won, the battle is the Lord's and I stand for Him to see His Kingdom come...*

If my journey today does not lead me to Jesus then I have traveled no further. Seeking after that one thing, Jesus said I am the way, the truth, the life. Now, I have become myself. Grace is free but the Kingdom will cost you everything...

Rebecca would be the first to say that God had appointed her seasons of struggle for her to go deeper in Him and to learn more about herself. Her eyes were opened to see unthought-of treasures in the Bible.

During times of struggle, Rebecca would be inspired by the beauty of God's creation. She loved butterflies and saw how the struggle a butterfly has to break free of its chrysalis, prepared it for the journey ahead.

Rebecca writes about butterfly migrations.

If the butterflies are taken off course, they find their way back to the right track/path/direction. God help me to choose the path of wisdom!

Rebecca gave God everything she had, heart and soul, and I can tell you she ran a great race and stayed on track.

Selah

I will give you treasures hidden in the darkness – secret riches. I will do this so you may know that I am the Lord... the one who calls you by name. (Isaiah 45:3, NLT)

Struggles are a normal part of a Christians walk and through them, God is growing your faith. In your own dark storms, search out the treasures God has for you through your struggles, not because of your circumstances but in spite of them. You may have wandered off the path but God is always there to carry you back.

What have you, or what are you, learning through your struggles?

Passing the Baton: Be strong and run with courage! Don't get discouraged, God is with you every step of the way.

Prayer: Dear Lord Jesus, please hear my prayer for help! I'm struggling with [tell God exactly you're your struggling with]. [If you need to, ask God to forgive you for anything you've done to hurt Him]. Please help and strengthen me to trust you and to fight the good fight of faith. Thank you for loving me and for the treasures you have promised to give me in the darkness. Amen.

Rebecca always encouraged young women to be humble and courageous to share their struggles with a tried and trusted Christian. Don't be alone in your struggles.

It's a New Day

Great is His faithfulness; his mercies begin afresh each morning. (Lamentations 3:23, NLT)

It's a new day. I have: new eyes, new mind, new heart, new ears, new desires...new manna each day, new mercies every single morning.

Rebecca's inner strength shines through her words. The glow of courage as she went from strength to strength, came at great cost after walking through a dark, wintry season of illness. The great sadness of grief and loss, her very busy life and her heart to serve others had left her physically and emotionally exhausted.

I pressed fast forward, so restless after Alex went home, almost couldn't stop to pause, suffering everywhere. I pray for the lost souls. The reality I once knew is suddenly something different, keep focused on God and keep praying. I will trust in who God says He is, rather than who I think He is.

Rebecca memorized scripture and hid God's word in her heart as a young girl. She was so grateful for the powerful word of God that was now sustaining her in this dark season. The Holy Spirit comforted her grieving heart and reminded her of God's promises.

She wrote,

I am so grateful for the love and prayers of my family, friends, wise Christian council and doctors, who have helped me through this dark season.

Selah

I hold you by your right hand – I, the Lord your God. And I say to you, "Don't be afraid. I am here to help you." (Isaiah 41:13, NLT)

For reasons only known to God, sometimes He takes us on a spiritual journey through painful seasons. Within the depth of the dark clouds, He is still close. Look for His treasures in the darkness and you will find them, as sure as the sunrise. His precious truth will bring light to your path and faith will rise and strengthen your heart. Trust that God will hold you no matter what!

Has pain, grief, loss, exhaustion, fear, doubt, loneliness or something else settled over you? If it has, share what you're going through with someone you trust, without delay.

Passing the Baton: Run with courage in the midst of the darkness and seek out the truth in God's word.

Rebecca's Prayer: *Dear Heavenly Father, I cry to you for help. Bring afresh to my heart your great love for me and let your grace carry me in this dark season. Thank you for your faithfulness and* *your new mercies offered to me each morning. Help me to find the treasures you have for me each day. Amen.*

While writing today's journal entry, a card arrived that was postmarked three weeks earlier by a dear friend. She included Lamentations 3:22-23, the same verse in our reading above!

Honoring Your Parents

Honor your father and mother. (Ephesians 6:2)

"Mum and Dad, thank you for your constant love and confidence in me, your encouragement and prayers just blow me away. I love you both very much and anything I've ever achieved is because of you and for you..." A portion of Rebecca's 21st Birthday speech that fell out of one of her journals.

Rebecca's 21st birthday party was a sparkling celebration. She not only shone in her own sweet way, gentle and humble, she glorified God by honoring us, with her beautiful expression of love and gratitude. At the time, I was moved to tears, as I am now, at Rebecca's heartfelt devotion, not only to us but to her Heavenly Father. She was a precious jewel in His crown and my darling daughter who I miss so much.

God created families to reflect His glory. Of course, all families have brief or seeming endless periods of struggle, but in whatever you are facing, hold on to God's command to honor your parents. When we honor our parents and love one another, we bring glory to God and welcome His presence into our family. We do not honor our parents because they deserve it; we honor them to glorify God by revealing His heart and plan for families.

I am thankful and blessed for the earthly family that God has given to me. I'm humbled and broken by the love I feel manifest through my family. I see

Jesus' sacrifice and I want to honor Him... I know who I am, I am a sinner saved by grace.

We grow in our relationship with God, and how we reflect Jesus, as we are obedient to His command to honor our parents.

As we obey Jesus' word, we show we are His disciples and then we really experience His truth and freedom.

Selah

Honor your father and mother – which is the first commandment with a promise – so that it may go well with you. (Ephesians 6:2-3)

Honor your parents. Express gratitude, make time for them, be considerate, let them into your life, speak kindly, forgive them and pray for them. These are just a few of many sweet and kind ways you can honor your parents.

It touches my heart when I read how Jesus honored His mother as He was dying on the cross.

What are some of the ways you can honor your father and mother?

Passing the Baton: Show your love for the Lord in the way you love and honor your parents.

Prayer: Dear Father God, please help me to live in pure obedience to you, full of your grace and truth. Please help me to glorify you by honoring my parents. I want to reveal your heart and plan for families. Thank you for your example in demonstrating such love in dying for me while I was still a sinner. Amen.

To Love is to be Vulnerable

Be kind to one another, tenderhearted, forgiving one another, as God in Christ forgave you. (Ephesians 4:32, NKJV)

"To love at all is to be vulnerable. Love anything and your heart will be wrung and possibly broken. If you want to make sure of keeping it intact you must give it to no one, not even an animal. Wrap it carefully round with hobbies and little luxuries, avoid all entanglements. Lock it up safe in the casket or coffin of your selfishness. But in the casket or coffin, safe, dark, motionless, airless, it will change. It will not be broken; it will become unbreakable, impenetrable, irredeemable. To love is to be vulnerable." C.S. Lewis

C.S. Lewis quotes are written throughout Rebecca's journals.

On her 21st birthday, Rebecca received a beautiful gift of pearls. She loved them so very much, not only because they were beautiful but also because they had been given to her by her Dad. A pearl is formed after an oyster opens up and a grain of sand embeds itself, and becomes uncomfortable inside its shell. The oyster embraces the object by covering it with many translucent layers. Over time a beautiful pearl is formed.

Jesus is the pearl of great price.

"We are not necessarily doubting that God will do the best for us; we are wondering how painful the best will turn out to be." C.S. Lewis. I saw this and it made me cry.'

To love is to risk EVERYTHING.

I'd rather love and risk than never feel. If I guarded my heart forever and never let another person in, it would be a dead life.

Love is a choice.

Love is surrender.

Love is a fight.

I choose to love because love is FREEDOM.

In her vulnerability, Rebecca found God's grace in new and deeper ways. She discovered a new freedom, praying and asking God to use her broken heart for His glory. God developed in her a tender heart that reached out and touched many people. She wrote,

No attack, no pearl.

Selah

As God's chosen people, holy and dearly loved, clothe yourselves with compassion, kindness, humility, gentleness and patience. Bear with each other and forgive one another if any of you has a grievance against someone. Forgive as the Lord forgave you. (Colossians 3:12-13)

God has created us to receive His love and to love Him in return and to love others. Because you have received God's love, you can be vulnerable as you love.

What is stopping you from being vulnerable in your love?

Passing the Baton: Be vulnerable as you love and allow God to form in you a tender heart.

Prayer: Heavenly Father, please help me to love other people even though it will make me vulnerable. And when people hurt me, help me to forgive them and to allow your love to heal my heart. Amen.

The Divine Potter

O Lord, you are our Father. We are the clay, and you are the potter. We all are formed by your hand. (Isaiah 64:8, NLT)

I surrender to your ways.

When Rebecca was a little girl, she loved to listen to her Dad tell her the stories from the Old Testament. They spoke to her sweet heart, and her trust in God's promises gave her strength for the days ahead.

She placed her life in the divine potter's hands and allowed Him to make something beautiful out of the furnace of her trials. Rebecca wrote,

I see the trials in my life as tests from God. That God is in control! I'm not!

One catastrophic trial was that suddenly and tragically, at the age of 24, Rebecca was told she was slowly losing her sight! She wrote,

O God! Let your hand mold me. I thank you that you are enough light for each step, even though I don't understand this. But I do understand the new things you have allowed me to see, one of which is, I am a great sinner and that Christ is a great savior. You know me best! You know what is best! I trust you with my life!

I watched Rebecca handle this unbelievable news with such grace, strength and dignity. She had a profound trust in God, no matter what she faced; it was always in her heart to give God the glory.

One of the many messages we received as a testament to Rebecca's life was:

"Rebecca's life sparkled. Most people didn't know of the difficulties she faced daily with her eyesight. I never sensed self-pity and she never complained or sought sympathy but lived with grace despite the challenges. Her positive attitude stood out."

We believed with Rebecca, that one day God would heal her eyes.

Selah

As the clay is in the potter's hand, so are you in mine. (Jeremiah 18:6, NLT)

Never, ever, give up! Instead of saying, "I can't believe that God would allow this," surrender your life into the hands of the divine potter. God is sovereign and He is in control. Whatever you are facing, you have the power to choose which direction your heart will take. Allow God to mold your life for something that will last forever and ever, to bring Him all the glory.

What do you need to surrender to the divine potter?

Passing the Baton: Even when you face disappointment or discouragement, run with grace, strength, beauty and dignity. Allow God to make something beautiful out of the furnace of your trials. He never let's go of you.

Rebecca's Prayer: *Dear Heavenly Father, I place my life in your hands and I ask that you would mold and make my heart sensitive to you - bend me! I ask for wisdom to know and accomplish the work you want me to do and to glorify your unmatched name through my life. Amen.*

Beautiful

He has made everything beautiful in its time...
(Ecclesiastes 3:11)

Rebecca's heart was touched by the truth of this verse and she wrote it in the shape of a heart in her journal and on the cards, she sent out. It was a truth she trusted and rested her life on.

Gentle reminders from Rebecca's journal:

God's timing is perfect! This is something easy to see, though difficult to understand. But, sometimes I wonder why it has taken so long for my eyes to open to see the way God works.

He controls time and is always on time. He is working in the world in how things happen.

There is a lot I am handing over to God. Although my heart has broken and life is hard, His love is sweet. It's His love that makes us and everything beautiful! God's timing is perfect and I know God will give beauty for ashes. Beautiful are the feet of those who bring good news.

My future is secure in Him. I see more than yesterday and I will see more tomorrow. I want to know the infinite one who walks with me. He has shown me the way to walk in righteousness. He has given me *the Holy Spirit, love, joy and peace take their place in my heart. I am thankful and eternally grateful.*

As I read Rebecca's words, I am missing her so much, but I do believe that her Father in Heaven called her home in His perfect timing.

I am humbled that you are reading this devotional and my prayer is that beauty will continue to rise up out of the ashes as you let Christ's light shine through you.

Selah

And we know that in all things God works for the good of those who love him, who have been called according to His purpose. (Romans 8:28)

If you've committed your life to Christ, God really does work "in all things" for you. God is in control of your circumstances and your life is in His hands, even when things happen that don't make any sense. In His providence, He is working 'in all things' to accomplish His eternal plan and purpose.

God has a plan for your life, and He is working to reveal more of Christ in and through you. Through the hard times and in the struggle, let hope arise and the beauty of Christ will shine through you.

How can you let the beauty of Christ shine through you?

Passing the Baton: Trust God to make all things beautiful in His time.

Prayer: Dear Heavenly Father, I'm sorry for the times I forget you are in control and that you hold all things in your powerful hand for my good and for your glory. Amen.

Temptations

The temptations in your life are no different from what others experience. And God is faithful. He will not allow the temptation to be more than you can stand. When you are tempted, he will show you a way out so that you can endure. (1 Corinthians 10:13, NLT)

Today I am wrestling with many things...I realize this is a fight of my faith...work at denying temptations... I want to honor God with my life. One thing I am grateful for is I am learning to fight against the lies from the enemy. I start with thanksgiving and ask the Holy Spirit to help me. I must quiet my mind, focus on God and be open to His voice. I will also read and meditate on His word.

I was reminded of a vision God gave me, it was of a person with their arms raised going through the finish line. I found that encouraging...The Key is to trust and obey, the battle is won...

The runner in Rebecca went into battle every day, fighting temptations in order to keep strong and fit for the race of life. She kept her mind on the word of God, remembering to pray, which is a key. By God's grace she fought the temptations, refusing to allow them to take her out of the race. It became her lifestyle. She wrote,

I want to be a fighter!...

Rebecca was a fighter and she lived a lifestyle that caused others to wonder and be inspired to follow Christ as she did.

Selah

For the grace of God has appeared that offers salvation to all people. It teaches us to say, "No" to ungodliness and worldly passions, and to live self-controlled, upright and godly lives in this world. (Titus 2:11-12)

Temptation starts in your mind and it only becomes a sin if you allow the enemy, and your own sinful desires, to entice you into wrong thoughts and action. The Bible teaches us to take our thoughts captive so that they do not produce sinful behavior.

Take captive every thought to make it obedient to Christ. (2 Corinthians 10:5)

Satan wants to take you out of the race, leaving you as a spectator. He wants to control your life and temptation is often very subtle. Keep alert and keep a Christ centered lifestyle. Pray to God for strength, by the Holy Spirit, to be self-controlled to say, 'No!' to things that are wrong. We cannot escape temptation, but we can choose to think and do what is right.

How do you prepare yourself to fight temptation?

Passing the Baton: Be a fighter! Do not let the enemy steel your sparkle, but live an attractive lifestyle, pointing people to Christ.

Prayer: Dear Heavenly Father, please fill me afresh with your Holy Spirit to strengthen my heart to be self-controlled and to say "No" to all temptations that lead me away from you. Amen.

I wrote this devotion on April 19th (Ben's birthday, Rebecca's brother) and, when I finished it, I read one of Rebecca's favorite devotionals, My Upmost for His Highest, by Oswald Chambers. Lo and behold, it fell open on April 19th, "Beware of the least likely temptation" 1 Corinthians 10:13! Thank you Lord for your sweet confirmation!

A Voice for the Voiceless

The Lord has anointed me to proclaim good news to the poor. He has sent me to bind up the brokenhearted, to proclaim freedom to the captives and release from darkness for the prisoners. (Isaiah 61:1)

Rebecca wrote an article for a Christian magazine,

It is our job to get as close to Jesus as possible... love the Lord your God with all your heart...so His Holy Spirit can work through us to reveal Jesus to others. We are Christ's beacons or ambassadors for the lost and hurting souls in this broken world. We are His eyes, ears, feet and voice.

Rebecca's heart for the hurting carries on through her journals,

I want to be a friend and a voice for the voiceless- slaves, prisoners, the poor, the unborn children, widows and orphans... I saw a circle of compassion and no-one was standing on the outside... we are to stand with those who hurt... we belong to one another.

The seeds of compassion were sown in Rebecca's heart when, as a young girl, she helped care for people in need with her parents in central London. On one occasion, she was moved to tears when she saw a photo of young girls who were held captive in a cage. She never forgot them and, as an adult, she joined the fight to stop human trafficking.

She also sponsored a young child, raised money for international justice, visited the poor and organized mission trips around the world to share the good news of Jesus Christ. Wanting to share God's love at Christmas time, she supported the families of prisoners, delivering gifts in person to the children.

Don't say you can help someone tomorrow if you can do it today. Tomorrow isn't promised!

Selah

For I was hungry and you gave me something to eat, I was thirsty and you gave me something to drink, I was a stranger and you invited me in, I needed clothes and you clothed me, I was sick and you looked after me, I was in prison and you came to visit me... Truly I tell you, whatever you did for one of the least of these brothers and sisters of mine, you did for me. (Matthew 25:35,36 and 40)

What breaks your heart? Does it ache for things that break God's heart?

Passing the Baton: Be a voice for the voiceless and be Jesus' hands and feet to the poor and suffering.

Prayer: Oh God! Please break my heart with the things that break your heart and give me the wisdom to know what to do and the courage to carry it through with loving kindness and truth. Amen.

Just as I was writing this devotional, our neighbor, who was unwell, knocked to ask if I could go food shopping for her. It wasn't convenient for me but hey, look what I was writing about!

Calling

For we are God's masterpiece. He has created us anew in Christ Jesus, so we can do the good things he planned for us long ago. (Ephesians 2:10, NLT)

Praying and meditating on God's word, Rebecca felt His heart for all the people who are "Lost," and His calling for her to be a witness to the youth. Shortly after, He graciously opened the door for her to be the National Director of Alpha Youth.

I'm privileged to support youth pastors and work with teen leaders and teen groups.

Every day I pray that God would save more souls to be with Him for eternity... Lord I feel so weak - please help me to glorify you in this new role.

One day every knee shall bow and every tongue confess that Jesus Christ is Lord. But until that day there is a work to do and a harvest waiting.

I feel God is pouring out His Spirit like never before, who's in for the one who paid it all? I am! Speaking to myself as I know many have seen this before me, but it's time to stand up! To speak up! Be a voice to our generation of the good News of our Savior Jesus Christ.

God has called those He has blessed to be a blessing, to shine brightly in the dark places of this world.

To weep with and help heal broken hearts with His love. To help heal wounds, to ultimately introduce the whole world to its precious Savior Jesus Christ.

I stop and weep in awe of Rebecca's beautiful and challenging words, written one year before she completed her race and was called home to Heaven.

She was obedient to God's calling and to the plan He had prepared for her long ago. The seeds she sowed continue to bear fruit in the lives of people today.

"I remember Rebecca always had a big smile on her face. She inspired and encouraged me to make a difference in the lives of young people. Rebecca, your legacy will live on in the hearts of so many, far and wide."

Selah

By the grace of God, I am what I am, and his grace to me was not without effect. (1 Corinthians 15:10)

You are God's masterpiece, and He will guide you into the plans and purposes He has prepared for you. As you step courageously into God's calling on your life, by His grace, He will equip you with everything you need to carry out His will and bring glory to His name.

Are you, "in for the one who paid it all?"

Passing the Baton: Be courageous in running the race He has called you to.

Prayer: Dear Heavenly Father, thank you that I am your masterpiece and that you have qualified me, and will give me the grace, to do the work you have called me to do. I commit myself to your calling for my life. Amen.

Tears

When Jesus saw her weeping... Jesus wept. (John 11:33 and 35)

I sense and feel in this season (and my life) God is working, God speaks to me in the tears. He is revealing deeper things to me and at times it is difficult to bear... I have felt a deep, deep pain in my heart for families who are suffering from the loss of loved ones, causing me to cry very much as I pray... let me bring hope and healing to show who Jesus Christ is, to bring His love. To be His hands and feet, to show His love to the world.

Rebecca's tears for her brother were heart changing. They became tears of compassion for others. Her tear-stained journals overflow with the cry of her heart. There is a fragrance of beauty about her journals, for Rebecca was weeping for lost and broken people. Tears, offered to God to be used for His glory.

Let me bring you glory in my valley, my valley of tears.

Rebecca journeyed on through her valley. As she wept for her brother, and for every hurting person, she sensed God was weeping too, for every lost and broken soul. It was while she grieved in God's presence, she received His grace and her strength was renewed to love and comfort others.

Just as Jesus wept, Rebecca was learning that true compassion is to comfort and suffer with others.

Weeping may endure for a night, but joy comes in the morning. This promise was a great comfort to me. He really does collect our tears.

With tears streaming down my face on the journey... allowing God to conform me to His will. To do the things He has planned for me to do... It has been tough and difficult but He is the God of all comfort and I am so very grateful to Jesus Christ for his healing touch...

Selah

Those who sow with tears will reap with songs of joy. Those who go out weeping, carrying seed to sow, will return with songs of joy, carrying sheaves with them. (Psalm 126:5-6)

Tears are a gift from God, allowing you to share heart to heart with Him. God is close to the broken hearted. Allow the Father of compassion and the God of all comfort to change your heart. With the comfort you have received, you will learn to comfort others. In this place of brokenness, He will renew your strength and guide you along the best path for your life, filled with His love and joy.

What do you feel God is saying to you through your tears?

Passing the Baton: Ask God to give you His heart for the "Lost" and for all who are suffering.

Prayer: Dear Heavenly Father, thank you for the gift of tears. You know and understand me and I ask you to please use every one of my tears to bring you glory. Thank you for being the God of all comfort, and please help and strengthen me to comfort others with the comfort you have given to me. Amen.

Romantic Love

Guard your heart above all else, for it is the source of life. (Proverbs 4:23, HCSB)

With a hard-romantic choice to be made, Rebecca wrote,

This morning, I'm asking God to give me strength and grace, to make the right choice, even if it's painful... Dear God, to be fully free in you, I want to lay my life down and say, I give you my dreams, my hopes, my desires, my heart.

Rebecca had told me that God had spoken to her in regards to a relationship. I remember her saying, "If He has spoken, will He not fulfill it?" She was going to trust God's promises, even in the area of her personal romantic decisions.

What is my passion? What is the one thing? To draw near to God with my whole heart and He will draw near to me.

Rebecca was always going to put Jesus first and she knew He was the only one that would ever be able to fill her heart. But, she did believe God had a soul mate for her, writing,

There is one my soul is tied to, since the beginning of time God arranged such a perfect union, no person can thwart God's perfect plan. I will wait, I will trust. He knows me better than anyone. He is my

best friend, He understands me... He is my helper and I am his forever, hearts as one (she drew a heart).

I believe her words for her future husband also give us a glimpse of our eternal bridegroom. I believe the spirit is always working to bring the bride of Christ to her bridegroom. Scripture tells us that the Church is the bride of Christ, and He is our bridegroom! At Rebecca's memorial, God mercifully carried me through with a vision of her as a beautiful bride meeting her bridegroom, with Alex close by.

Selah

For this reason, a man will leave his father and mother and be united to his wife, and the two will become one flesh. This is a profound mystery but I am talking about Christ and the church. (Ephesians 5:31-32)

One day, we will all meet our Heavenly bridegroom, our Savior, who is perfect in every way. He is the one we should desire above all others. He is the only one who fully completes and satisfies the deepest longing of our soul. Jesus is the only perfect one who will never let us down.

What is your passion? What is your one thing?

Passing the Baton: Guard your heart because out of it flows the well spring of life.

Prayer: Dear Lord Jesus, I adore you. Thank you for your love for me. You are the lover of my soul and my heart rejoices in you. Help me to trust you and to allow you to take full possession of my heart. My beloved is mine and I am His, and His banner over me is love. Amen.

Laughter

She is clothed with strength and dignity; she can laugh at the days to come. (Proverbs 31:25)

Where did Rebecca's strength come from?

It comes from within, as I seek God with all my heart...

Rather like running in a race, Rebecca would seek God with expectancy and eager anticipation as she read and meditated over her Bible, prayed and worshipped God. It was while she was waiting on God that she clothed herself with strength.

Rebecca's lifestyle demonstrated the triumph of the grace of God in every area of her life and she endured with such dignity. Because she knew and trusted God, she was free to *laugh at the days to come.* Rebecca was definitely not afraid, writing,

I don't even know what tomorrow holds, I just know God holds me and that's enough!

Enjoy life to the full! This morning I enjoyed just being together with friends, talking, laughing enjoying each other and listening to beautiful music by Bach...

Today has been another gift from God, precious and joyful, I see God has put great blessings into my life: love, joy, peace, friends and family...

Rebecca's best friends from her high school in London sent us a beautiful and thoughtful gift. They had painted a picture of a tree, and its branches were laden with precious memories of Rebecca. One of them read, "Laughing so hard it made her eyes water!" That was our Rebecca, she laughed like she meant it – such an infectious laugh!

Selah

A cheerful heart is good medicine. (Proverbs 17:22)

Laughter and our sense of humor are gifts from God. There is a time for everything and a season for every activity under Heaven, a time to weep and a time to laugh.

Are you free enough to laugh at the days to come? Who could you bless with some fun and laughter today?

Passing the Baton: Receive strength in your quiet time with God, and laugh at the days to come.

Prayer: Dear Lord Jesus, thank you so much for the gift of laughter that refreshes my soul and brings light and lightness to my day. Help me to bring laughter and joy to those you bring into my life. Amen.

Angels

For he will order his angels to protect you wherever you go. (Psalm 91:11, NLT)

Rebecca was very adventurous (taking after her Dad), and I always prayed for God's protection over her. However, after Rebecca went home to Heaven, I was faced with the question, "Do I really believe in God's promise to protect us wherever we go?"

Through the overwhelming suffering of a mother's broken heart, God answered my question and revealed to me many spiritual realities of things we don't normally see. Rebecca's guardian angels did protect her throughout her life and every moment of her life was laid out before a single day had passed (Psalm 139:16). Although I can hardly breathe for sorrow and I miss my girl and my boy, I can say with full assurance, May 8th 2014 was the day that God had planned to call Rebecca home. He did not leave her or forsake her; He ordered her guardian angels to carry her safely home and into His arms.

Rebecca's own words on angels are comforting to me and speak of her absolute faith and trust in God.

God has His Heavenly armies encamped around us... The Lord has promised to watch out for me and protect me, my future is secure in Him. Thinking to myself, I am faced with a strange set of realities, one sees only about a third of what is actually going on! The realities of the spiritual world are evident and active here on Earth. God is always working for His perfect plan and purpose.

Rebecca chose, *Same Kind of Different as Me*, for her book club.

I was so moved reading, Same Kind of Different as Me, a story of redemption that touched my heart. I felt I'd like to buy a painting of, "Angels in Disguise" by the homeless man in the story.

In the days after Rebecca went home, remembering how touched she had been by the story, I would stare with tear filled eyes at the painting, "Angels in Disguise." I thought about Jesus in the Garden of Gethsemane before his crucifixion. Yielding to His Father's will, an angel appeared to Him and strengthened Him. I prayed that God would also strengthen me.

In those moments, I thought of something Rebecca said to me a lot, *"Keep your eyes on Jesus!"*

God's angels really do appear in different forms and when we least expect. Sometimes angels even come as people.

Selah

Angels are only servants – spirits sent to care for people who will inherit salvation. (Hebrews 1:14, NLT)

God's angels are sent to protect you and one day bring you safely home, where you will hear the voice of many angels numbering thousands upon thousands worshipping and singing, "Worthy is the Lamb who was slain, to receive power and wealth and wisdom and strength and honor and glory and praise." May we live to praise Jesus Christ and never the angels.

What is God illuminating to you from this message?

Passing the Baton: Run courageously, knowing that God has ordered His angels to protect you.

Prayer: Heavenly Father, thank you for creating angels and for the many ways they help and look after us. I'm grateful for how they protect and help me on my journey. Amen.

Heaven

Set your sights on the realities of Heaven... Think about the things of Heaven not the things of Earth. (Colossians 3:1-2, NLT)

The Bible teaches that Heaven is our true home, while our time on Earth is only temporary. It begs the question, though, how often do we really think about Heaven? But when someone you love dies, you do begin to wonder about the things of Heaven. Rebecca had this very experience, when her brother Alex went home. Part of her heart went with him, and knowing this was not the end of the story, she chose to meditate on the Bible's truth about Heaven. Rebecca wrote,

I have family in Heaven and on Earth...

Live for the treasures of Heaven, don't worry about uncertainties...

An expression of her strong faith was when she would say to me, "I wonder what Alex is doing now?" In Heaven, all mysteries will be revealed, but until then, we agreed that Alex is enjoying the glory of God in his true home. He has joined the great cloud of witnesses and is worshipping Jesus in a perfect place; a place free of pain, perfect peace and joy and pleasures for evermore. We liked to think that he is running – but one can only imagine!

Rebecca loved to paint and, as a gift, she painted the beautiful bouquet of roses that her Dad bought me for our wedding anniversary. Written above one of the roses was Ecclesiastes 3:11.

God has made everything beautiful in its time. He has planted eternity in the human heart.

This verse means more to me than words can say because, only a month later my heart was broken again when my precious Rebecca was also called home to Heaven!

Rebecca brought glory to God by finishing the work He had given her here on Earth. She crossed the finish line and, after embracing Jesus, I like to imagine that Alex was waiting to give her a welcome home hug, caught up in joy, worshipping God with family, friends and heroes of the faith. One day we will all be together again, with no one missing.

Selah

Store up for yourselves treasures in heaven... for where your treasure is, there your heart will be also. (Matthew 6:20-21)

The Bible teaches that how we live our lives on Earth will be rewarded in Heaven. Relative to eternity, we have so few years to live out God's unique calling for us and if we miss that, we miss everything. Run the rest of your life with perseverance, fixing your eyes on Jesus. The most important thing is that by welcoming Jesus into your heart, you know you're going to Heaven. To miss your invitation to Heaven, would be the greatest tragedy of all.

What can you do differently today to start investing in Heaven?

Passing the Baton: Store up treasure in Heaven by being faithful to His calling.

If you want to be sure that you will go to Heaven when you die, please consider saying the prayer below.

"Lord Jesus, I'm sorry for all the wrong things I've done. Thank you for dying on the cross for me to forgive my sins and I invite you to come into my heart and be Lord of my life. Thank you for giving me the gift of eternal life and please fill my heart with your pure love. Amen."

If you have already given your heart to Jesus, pray the following prayer:

Dear Lord Jesus, thank you that you will make all things beautiful in its time and that you have set eternity in my heart. You are the only one that can satisfy my soul and please help me to run the race you have marked out for me. Amen.

Shortly after he went home, the God of all comfort gave me a vision of Alex that has forever changed my understanding of Heaven. I prayed that I might also see

Rebecca, and God answered my prayer through a friend, who saw Rebecca in a dream and she was radiant. God was gracious in answering my prayers, because I never had a chance to say goodbye to my precious Rebecca and Alex.